POETRY STARS

A Treasure Trove Of Poetry

Edited By Roseanna Caswell

First published in Great Britain in 2023 by:

YoungWriters® Est. 1991

Young Writers
Remus House
Coltsfoot Drive
Peterborough
PE2 9BF
Telephone: 01733 890066
Website: www.youngwriters.co.uk

All Rights Reserved
Book Design by Ashley Janson
© Copyright Contributors 2022
Softback ISBN 978-1-80459-340-0

Printed and bound in the UK by BookPrintingUK
Website: www.bookprintinguk.com
YB0530C

FOREWORD

Welcome to a fun-filled book of poems!

Here at Young Writers, we are delighted to introduce our new poetry competition for KS1 pupils, Poetry Stars. Pupils could choose to write an acrostic, sense poem or riddle to introduce them to the world of poetry. Giving them this framework allowed the young writers to open their imaginations to a range of topics of their choice, and encouraged them to include other literary techniques such as similes and description.

From family and friends, to animals and places, these pupils have shaped and crafted their ideas brilliantly, showcasing their budding creativity in verse.

We live and breathe creativity here at Young Writers – it gives us life! We want to pass our love of the written word onto the next generation and what better way to do that than to celebrate their writing by publishing it in a book!

Each awesome little poet in this book should be super proud of themselves, and now they've got proof of their imagination and their ideas when they first started creative writing to look back on in years to come! We hope you will delight in these poems as much as we have.

CONTENTS

Bantock Primary School, Pennfields

David Audu (8)	1
Milana Bailey (8)	2
Caley Nanga (8)	4
Gurnoor Singh (8)	5

EDS Writers' Club, Crowthorne

Chanudi Adhikari (8)	6

Fryent Primary School, Fryent

Melek Karrar Shaker Al-Mosawi (8)	7
Karen Xu (10)	8
Kiara Brown-Rummun (10)	10
Nadia Haidary (11)	12
Kashwin Mohanaruban (6)	14
Zuhairah Ahmad (8)	15
Hana Harghandewal (6)	16
Achmad Muchlis (6)	17
Lilly-Grace Haynes (8)	18
Bianca Maria Bologan (10)	19
Anastasia Lung (5)	20
Rafia Ali (8)	21
Danielle Ikuesan (6)	22
Dimitar Dimitrov (10)	23
Ali Tanveer Daroge (8)	24
Rhea-May Critchley (10)	25
Anaaya Nagiah (9)	26
Stephany Romoli Santana (8)	27
Alecsia Elena Radescu (9)	28
Amos Bejenar (7)	29
Isabella Maria Lupaescu (8)	30
Corey Mason Ashley Hunt (8)	31

Mohamad Zakariya Khan (8)	32
Mandana Ghavami (5)	33
Thea Olteanu (6)	34
Tashauna Jada White (11)	35
Amaya Noor Naeem (9)	36
Zayn Ali Khan (8)	37
Rebeca Motac (7)	38
Gabriel Dica (9)	39
Harum Nowsharwan (5)	40
Mohammad Arshman Riaz (8)	41
Tavona Algama (5)	42
Ionut Alex (9)	43
Farhat Parwani (5)	44
Mya Patel (6)	45
Rosie-Mea Patel (6)	46
Suraya Sampaney (6)	47
Safa Rageh (7)	48
Agnes Popa (8)	49
Bilal Mohamed (5)	50
Hadiya Alamyar (7)	51
Mohamed Hassan (8)	52
Anvika Date (9)	53
Sarah Iman Rana (6)	54
Yusuf Reja (7)	55
Sarah Hendricks (6)	56
Milen Patel (9)	57
Abdulrahman Mohammed (5)	58
Jalpa Vekariya (6)	59
Hadi Alashkar (6)	60
Tanay Hirani (6)	61
Salem Al-Salem (6)	62
Noor Javed (6)	63
Abigail Motac (6)	64
Sofia Rotaru (7)	65
Charlie Harris (7)	66

Alexandros Alex Tzatzo (8)	67
Aya Albuarabi (5)	68
Mariyah Qamer (6)	69
Fraya Kashvi Patel (4)	70

Heene CE (A) Primary School, Worthing

Tudor Alexandru Timofte (9)	71

Ripley Endowed CE Primary School, Ripley

Ava B (8)	72
Albert S (8)	73
Freya Slater (7)	74
Lewis W (8)	75
Olivia P (8)	76

Smallwood Primary School, Tooting

Mariyam Syeda	77
Annabelle How (8)	78
Sheema Syeda	80
Arshiya Syeda	82
Ariz Vahora (7)	84
Khalid Peart (8)	85
Oliver Cumming (7)	86
Janine Takawira (7)	87
Harlow Rodney (8)	88
Benedict Lort-Phillips (7)	89
Oliver Gulliford (7)	90
Sam Marsh (7)	91
Esme Lewis-Crosby	92
Chloe Callaby (7)	93
Dylan Ingram-Richardson (7)	94
Iraj Nasir (7)	95
Aman Malik (7)	96
Kamran Qadeer (7)	97
Kristian Mitrev (7)	98

St Mary's CE (VA) Primary School, Portbury

Kamva Sowati (9)	99
Josh Jenkins (9)	100
Rebecca Poole (8)	101
Seb Johnson (7)	102
Jacob Baylis (7)	103
Shana Bateman (7)	104
Imogen Speed (5)	105
Eva Ahern (6)	106
Sebastian Purcell (8)	107
Esme Smith (6)	108
Charlie Ferguson (6)	109
Marika Korbien (8)	110
Jacob Thomson (8)	111
Charlotte Corr (9)	112
Emilia Bundy (7)	113
Ezra Jones (7)	114
Freya Larder (6)	115
Lochy Batt (5)	116
Amelia Burke (7)	117
Bella Poole (6)	118
Devon Dempsey (6)	119
Arran Batt (6)	120
Max Hill (8)	121
Edith Dean (7)	122
Saul Chalkley (6)	123
Lamar Ali (9)	124
Max Joyner (7)	125
Aneirin Guttridge (5)	126

St Wilfrid's Catholic Primary School, Ashton In Makerfield

Layla Morgan (7)	127
Mia Pasquill (6)	128
Lucy Carson (6)	129
Benjamin Pennington (6)	130
Ksawier Pitucha (7)	131
Kasper Ballard (6)	132
Freddie Ballard (6)	133
Olivia Smith (6)	134
Mason Olori (6)	135

Logan Sheridan (6)	136
Ella Easton (6)	137
Sylvie Smith (6)	138
Blake Thorpe (6)	139
Molly Armstrong-Storey (6)	140
Leo Stott (6)	141

THE POEMS

Happiness

H appy to hang out with my friend
A lways happy
P uffy is with my friends
P uffy is my favourite animal
I have friends
N ever angry
E very day is a good day
S tuff makes me happy
S ongs make me feel better.

David Audu (8)
Bantock Primary School, Pennfields

Hey!

Hey Mom, I am here to say I am sorry for having a meltdown yesterday
Hey Dad, I am here to say I love you and this is my life with you
Hey friend, I am here to say I'm sorry for fighting you, although you got me mad, I still forgive you
Hey brother, I am so sorry for sneaking into your room, I promise I will stay out of your room
Hey aunt, I am here to apologise for what I did last night, it was the wrong thing to do
Hey teacher, I am here to say thank you for having me in your classroom
Hey uncle, I am so sorry for messing up your new house, I am here to say I will tidy it up now
Hey, I have a pet cat and it is strong, you do not want to go by it, it is dangerous

Hey sister, I am here to say sorry
Hey, do you know that sea creatures are in the ocean?
Hey, do you know that clouds move?
Hey, do you know that the river goes on forever?

Milana Bailey (8)
Bantock Primary School, Pennfields

Oh, What A Queen

Reigning for 70 years
Training for all her life
Has been a great wife
A great mother
Always smothers her child with kisses
Her hallways are prolonged
She now belongs to God
She has two dogs
They have jobs to make a mess
But people are obsessed.

Caley Nanga (8)
Bantock Primary School, Pennfields

About My Best Aunty

A diamanté poem

Aunty
Caring, kind
Cooking, playing, reading
Pasta, flower, dog, books
Helping, studying, travelling
Smiling, pink
Nephew.

Gurnoor Singh (8)
Bantock Primary School, Pennfields

Candyland

C andyland is a sweet, delicious place for all
A pples dipped in candy sauce and sprinkled with gumdrops
N ecklaces made out of scrumptious candy, filled with lots of chocolate
D elicate strips of sour cherry candy, packed with flavour
Y es to all the yummy sweets
L anding in a place with brightness and joy
A valanches full of candy, roll down the hill
N est of chocolate birds, feeding their babies caramel dips
D rizzling with chocolate sauce everywhere.

Chanudi Adhikari (8)
EDS Writers' Club, Crowthorne

Nuts

I'm small and my food is with me in a tree
My favourite branch is short and wide
And strong for me to sleep on
I go around to other trees
But I always come to my special one
Before midnight when no one can find me
I am not a carnivore, I am a herbivore
All the branches are too spiky for me
Just my one is smooth and comfortable
I collect food for winter
Don't try to catch me because I will
blaze past
I have lovely cousins called Chip and Dale
My skin is brown and my tail is a bit bushy
What am I?

Answer: A squirrel.

Melek Karrar Shaker Al-Mosawi (8)
Fryent Primary School, Fryent

The Swamp

As I tumbled through the swamp
Strange sounds, scents and plants surrounded me

In the distance I could hear birds chirping
And the smell of fresh grass
Drifted through the air

Bees were huddling in a clover
Buzzing noisily at each other
Great big mucky bogs stuck firmly on the ground
Sucking any insect that lays a foot on them
I wonder, could it be strong enough to suck a human down?

I can see a carpet of damp tall trees
With slender white branches towering into the sky
Like an overgrown cursed plant

I could feel the thick, humid air slapping my face
As I flicked a mosquito off my eyebrow
I felt hot and itchy

Then I walked up to a small, oval-shaped pond
The water was dark green
Floating on top were elegant, white water lilies bending over flat green lilypads
What a stunning, attractive sight!

Karen Xu (10)
Fryent Primary School, Fryent

Climate Change

The beam of light peeping through the clouds, greeting us every morning
Appears to be getting hotter every year
Triggering wildfires, making the land feel vulnerable
Is global warming possibly near?

The sea is a flood of tears
From the creatures suffering as their home, we polluted
A calming still turned into a wave of rage
Plastic and oil... the creature's happiness we looted

The towering trees glancing down at us
Habitat to many animals, we continue to chop
What is more important, the paper or the air we breathe?
We continue to harm our environment, it needs to stop

As a community, we should unlike
Land, sea and creatures we should embrace
Let's do our best to refresh our home
Make the world a better place.

Kiara Brown-Rummun (10)
Fryent Primary School, Fryent

The Earth Is Calling

The Earth is calling day by day
But nobody seems to say, "Hey!"
Each and every night, Mother Nature
Hopes not to see our world in danger
Trees on fire, houses falling
But all they say is, "Oh no! Oh no!
Our world isn't the same!"
Old times and new, both shouldn't be true
Earth is calling
Earth is calling
Waiting on us to make a change
As it watches in dismay
Every little thing makes a difference
Keeping the rivers clean
Keeping the fresh air we breathe
Keeping the forest green
Each and every one of us can take time
On any day to show the Earth we care

Remember there is always a solution
To our problem is we do our part
And make a revolution.

Nadia Haidary (11)
Fryent Primary School, Fryent

Sense Of The Seasons

My sight of the green glossy trees
Swaying here and there with peace
The summer sun is pouring its light
Animals searching for food with a fight

The aroma of the pretty pink flowers
Perfuming the air for the followers
Monkeys are the followers
Monkeys are searching for fruit
In all the different forest routes

The rushing levels are whispering
Telling the animals to go into hibernation
Winter is on its way
All the animals are running away.

Kashwin Mohanaruban (6)
Fryent Primary School, Fryent

Beautiful Creature

I have too many horns that kinda look like a bone
My whole body is spotty like a ladybird
I might be the second-tallest animal in the world
I sometimes live in a safari and sometimes in a zoo
I can tell you now that I'm not a carnivore
I know that I don't have a sharp nose
I have so many fleas around my body
I have a purple tongue
What am I?

Answer: A giraffe.

Zuhairah Ahmad (8)
Fryent Primary School, Fryent

I Can...

When I go outside, I can see the sky
It looks like the ocean at the seaside

I can also feel the sunlight
It feels cosy and warm, such a delight

I can also taste the rain
To my surprise, it doesn't taste that plain

I can smell the air
It smells fresh and feels good in my hair

I can also feel the grass with my feet
I think it's something everyone needs.

Hana Harghandewal (6)
Fryent Primary School, Fryent

Sweetcorn

S weetcorn is sweet
W ater makes sweetcorn grow
E verybody loves sweetcorn
E verybody should try sweetcorn because it is yummy
T rees are plants like corn
C orn is the same as popcorn
O ranges are tasty like sweetcorn and popcorn
R ain helps the plants to grow and the plants make sweetcorn
N ew things are corn.

Achmad Muchlis (6)
Fryent Primary School, Fryent

Pollution

P eople not putting rubbish in the bin
O ur lungs filled with polluted air
L itter in our rivers and oceans
L ove for this earth not valued
U nnecessary animals' deaths
T his earth is a beautiful place
I want to make a change
O il now flowing into rivers
N ow is the time to change this!

Lilly-Grace Haynes (8)
Fryent Primary School, Fryent

Climate Change

Once upon a time
Our world was looking
So beautiful and neat
But now everywhere
There is rubbish, paper
And plastic is found in every bush
That is bad for the animals
That live in the oceans or everywhere
They can die
Everyone needs to save the world
To save everyone
Then we can live on a good Earth
And not a bad Earth.

Bianca Maria Bologan (10)
Fryent Primary School, Fryent

Ice Cream

I ce cream is cold
C old like the South Pole
E veryone loves ice cream

C reamy and smooth, it melts on a hot day
R ed is for strawberry and blue is for blueberry
E very week, I go to the park and get an ice cream
A mazing, cool while it melts in my mouth
M y favourite treat is ice cream.

Anastasia Lung (5)
Fryent Primary School, Fryent

Significant Sea Creature

One of my species is the largest on Earth
I live in saltwater and eat tiny sea creatures
I need to spew water out to survive
If you're on a boat you will see me trying to greet you
By jumping straight out of my home
I love to travel
What am I?

Answer: A whale.

Rafia Ali (8)
Fryent Primary School, Fryent

Summer

In summer, I can see the beautiful sea
I can see the bright sun shining in the sky
I can smell the air
I can smell the barbecues in the gardens
I can taste ice cream and pop cakes
I can hear people dancing, playing to the beat of the music
Summer feels hot
Summer is fun.

Danielle Ikuesan (6)
Fryent Primary School, Fryent

Protect Nature

The wind blows nature to look free
We love to see the sky, trees and sun shout, "Wee!"
We are all humans and like wildlife, we have fun and run
Hurting nature one by one but we are too relaxed staring at the sun
But it's not so simple to spot the mistakes and see.

Dimitar Dimitrov (10)
Fryent Primary School, Fryent

The Night Hunter

I live in the dark woods
I take advantage of the time
I'm furry and sly with great eyesight
I have jagged teeth
I make you have more than a heartbeat
I will chase you as fast as a pro can hit a baseball
I have razor-sharp claws on my paws
What am I?

Ali Tanveer Daroge (8)
Fryent Primary School, Fryent

Summer Love

Scorching hot sun, shining so bright
The sky is ocean blue, and clouds
are dreamy white
Ice cream, barbecues, sun-kissed tans
The smell of sun lotion all over my hands
Half term is here! Yes, six weeks of fun
Let's make the most of the British sun.

Rhea-May Critchley (10)
Fryent Primary School, Fryent

Slithering Long

I have a long, slithery body
My tongue is as wide as a knife
I slither in the long grass so you never catch me
I don't have a family so I'm homeless
I can escape but you'll never catch me
What am I?

Answer: A snake.

Anaaya Nagiah (9)
Fryent Primary School, Fryent

An Eating Machine

I am a brown animal that likes playing
I make a weird noise
I like to eat yellow things
I eat and drink in a tree
You can find me in an animal zoo
Probably all the bananas will be gone because of me
What am I?

Answer: A monkey.

Stephany Romoli Santana (8)
Fryent Primary School, Fryent

A Woolly Four-Legged Animal

I can make weird noises
People use me to make clothes
I can be dyed different colours
Farmers use me and I am kept in a den
I am fleecy so pet me as much as you please
I munch on grass all day
What am I?

Answer: A sheep.

Alecsia Elena Radescu (9)
Fryent Primary School, Fryent

What Am I?

I am white and sometimes colourful
I have sharp edges too
You can cut me or fold me
You can read me or dispose of me
But don't forget to recycle me
Because we must be environmentally friendly
What am I?

Answer: Paper.

Amos Bejenar (7)
Fryent Primary School, Fryent

The Impossible Riddle

I am scary to some people
But I'm actually very fascinating
I live everywhere
Some people think I'm an insect but I'm not
I only eat meat so I'm a carnivore
I am very hairy
What am I?

Answer: A spider.

Isabella Maria Lupaescu (8)
Fryent Primary School, Fryent

The Sly Animal

I am a very fluffy animal
You can find me in the freezing Arctic
My fur is white
I'm very sly but not much
I hunt to stay alive
I'm very cute but think twice... I can bite
I'm not a wolf
I'm very cool
What am I?

Corey Mason Ashley Hunt (8)
Fryent Primary School, Fryent

What Am I?

I fly like a bird
I eat food off the ground
When I am on the ground I am slow
I look for food because my tummy rumbles all the time
I am soft
I am friendly
I have sharp claws
What am I?

Answer: A vulture.

Mohamad Zakariya Khan (8)
Fryent Primary School, Fryent

Mandana

M andana has a magnificent heart
A beautiful girl
N obody dislikes
D oor to a beautiful world
A pure heart for a beautiful world
N ow a beautiful and smart girl
A warrior for the world.

Mandana Ghavami (5)
Fryent Primary School, Fryent

Mother Baking A Cake

I look through the kitchen window
And I see my mother is baking a cake
I can smell its sweetness
And I am ready to taste
I am going inside to ask for a slice
Be patient, little one
Don't touch the oven, it's not very wise.

Thea Olteanu (6)
Fryent Primary School, Fryent

Year Six

I've now left Year Five, it's time for Year Six
Here comes the SATs and the harder maths
But still, I'm focusing on reaching the top
Hard work and dedication and I know
I can't stop because my desire is to be at the top!

Tashauna Jada White (11)
Fryent Primary School, Fryent

My Animal Riddle

I am really fluffy
I like vegetables
I have big ears and legs
My face is very tiny
I love to hop around a lot
You can find me in different colours
White, brown and peach
What am I?

Answer: A rabbit.

Amaya Noor Naeem (9)
Fryent Primary School, Fryent

The Unthinkable Riddle

I have razor-sharp teeth
I am very cute
I am always on trees that are high
I roll around when I'm asleep
I am as small as a rabbit
I love to eat huge leaves like a sloth
I am very furry and soft
What am I?

Zayn Ali Khan (8)
Fryent Primary School, Fryent

What Am I?

I am white
I can be colourful
You can bend me
You can draw on me
You can stick on me
I am flat
You cannot eat me
You can trim me
You can put stuff on me
What am I?

Answer: Paper.

Rebeca Motac (7)
Fryent Primary School, Fryent

I Want To Be...

I want to be a footballer
I want to be so happy
I want to shine like a star
Someone like Ronaldo

I will work enough to be a star
With lots of sacrifice
But in the end...
I will be like...
Ronaldo.

Gabriel Dica (9)
Fryent Primary School, Fryent

Fryent

F ryent is the best
R espect is the key to success
Y ou have to be sensible
E verybody has to be responsible
N ice children are always cool
T eachers are the best in my school.

Harum Nowsharwan (5)
Fryent Primary School, Fryent

What Am I?

I am sharp but I'm not edible
You can put me on your walls
You can stick me
You can draw on me
You can write on me too
I can help you learn
What am I?

Answer: Paper.

Mohammad Arshman Riaz (8)
Fryent Primary School, Fryent

Watermelon

I wash my hands
I see a cat
My name is Tavona
I eat eggs
I run into the park
My mum is a super girl
I like elephants
I like my toys
I like oranges
I see the birds next.

Tavona Algama (5)
Fryent Primary School, Fryent

A Corn-Eater Machine

I eat corn and hay
I make food for other people
I am hairy to touch
I stay in a barn
I don't clean myself
I make the sound of oink
What am I?

Answer: A pig.

Ionut Alex (9)
Fryent Primary School, Fryent

Farhat

F ootball is fun
A nd basketball is boring to me
R ugby is very hard
H ockey is easy
A nd I have one fun sport
T hat is tennis because it is fun.

Farhat Parwani (5)
Fryent Primary School, Fryent

Winter

I can see bold white snow
I can hear snowballs crashing and children giggling
I can taste the water from the snowflakes
I can feel the cold ground
I can smell the warm, yummy soup.

Mya Patel (6)
Fryent Primary School, Fryent

Solar Power

S un
O cean
L andscape
A mazon
R e-usable

P ollution
O zone layer
W astage
E nergy
R ecycle.

Rosie-Mea Patel (6)
Fryent Primary School, Fryent

The Beach

I can see rocky cliffs
I can hear water splashing
I can taste yummy ice cream
I can feel the wet sand
I can smell salty water
I can go crabbing
I love the beach.

Suraya Sampaney (6)
Fryent Primary School, Fryent

The White Stuff

I have no feelings
My colour is white
You can fold me
I am inedible
I am a rectangle shape
People stick stuff on me
What am I?

Answer: Paper.

Safa Rageh (7)
Fryent Primary School, Fryent

What Am I?

I like playing with my owner
I am black and white
I have soft fur
I have green eyes
I like playing with my toys
What am I?

Answer: A dog.

Agnes Popa (8)
Fryent Primary School, Fryent

Cake

C hocolate yummy cake
A mazingly melting in my mouth
K eep eating until I finish it all
E xtremely delicious, I can't wait to have more.

Bilal Mohamed (5)
Fryent Primary School, Fryent

What Am I?

I am white and you draw on me
If you don't recycle me
then you might forget about me
You might get cut by me
What am I?

Answer: Paper.

Hadiya Alamyar (7)
Fryent Primary School, Fryent

Dangerous Mythical Animal

I am warm not cold or hot
I am big but not as big as the sun
I am as big as the moon
I have elemental powers
I have fangs and not teeth
What am I?

Mohamed Hassan (8)
Fryent Primary School, Fryent

Autumn And Spring

A diamanté poem

Autumn
Leaves, fall
Changing, admiring, falling
Shades, ombre, flower, photosynthesis
Planting, cleaning, budding
Fresh, fun
Spring.

Anvika Date (9)
Fryent Primary School, Fryent

The Beach

I can smell the fresh air
I can see the ocean
I can hear people having fun
I can touch the grainy sand
I can taste the lovely fish and chips.

Sarah Iman Rana (6)
Fryent Primary School, Fryent

What Am I?

I am white
You can fold me
I am a rectangle
You can destroy me with water
You can rip me
What am I?

Answer: Paper.

Yusuf Reja (7)
Fryent Primary School, Fryent

Rainy Summer Day

The rain is going in the flowers
The butterflies are flying
The sun is shining bright
The people are having fun
In the park all day long.

Sarah Hendricks (6)
Fryent Primary School, Fryent

Dark And Light

A diamanté poem

Dark
Creepy, gloomy
Dreaming, sleeping, gazing
Sleep, relax, garden, birds
Playing, jogging, raining
Free, natural
Light.

Milen Patel (9)
Fryent Primary School, Fryent

Earth

E arth is the best planet
A lways keep safe
R ecycle all things
T ogether we can
H elp save Earth.

Abdulrahman Mohammed (5)
Fryent Primary School, Fryent

The Seaside

I can see fish and sand
I can hear waves and the cool breeze
I can smell ice cream and the ocean
I can taste fish and salty hot dogs.

Jalpa Vekariya (6)
Fryent Primary School, Fryent

My Senses

I can see the snows
I can hear the crows
I can feel with my hands and toes
I can smell with my nose
I can taste some Slushie.

Hadi Alashkar (6)
Fryent Primary School, Fryent

The Seaside

I can hear the noisy kids
I can see small crabs
I can smell the salty water
I can feel the fresh air
I can taste candyfloss.

Tanay Hirani (6)
Fryent Primary School, Fryent

Ocean Seas

I can hear the waves
I can see dolphins
I can taste the salty water
I can smell the fishy odour
I can touch a starfish.

Salem Al-Salem (6)
Fryent Primary School, Fryent

The Seaside

I can see people
I can smell fish and chips
I can hear barking dogs
I can feel the cool water
I can taste cotton candy.

Noor Javed (6)
Fryent Primary School, Fryent

The Seaside

I can see sand
I can smell ice cream
I can hear kids screaming
I can feel grainy sand
I can taste cotton candy.

Abigail Motac (6)
Fryent Primary School, Fryent

The Seaside

I can see boats
I can hear waves
I can smell the salty water
I can taste ice cream
I can feel the cool water.

Sofia Rotaru (7)
Fryent Primary School, Fryent

Natural Riddle

I am green and brown
I live in nature
Apples grow on me
What am I?

Answer: An apple tree.

Charlie Harris (7)
Fryent Primary School, Fryent

What Am I?

I am flat
You can fold me
You can put me in the bin
What am I?

Answer: Paper.

Alexandros Alex Tzatzo (8)
Fryent Primary School, Fryent

Cake

The cake is yummy
Aya loves them
I love cake with chocolate
And sprinkles
Cake, cake, cake!

Aya Albuarabi (5)
Fryent Primary School, Fryent

The Seaside

I can see the clear cool sea
I can hear beautiful birds
I can hear them chirping.

Mariyah Qamer (6)
Fryent Primary School, Fryent

Bedtime

I went to bed
Jumping up and down
I fell and bumped my head.

Fraya Kashvi Patel (4)
Fryent Primary School, Fryent

Christmas Is Coming

C hristmas, Christmas, Christmastime is coming
H appiness and cheer are in the air
R ight time for Christmas decorations, shops
I ce starts to fall as Christmas comes
S taying inside, it's too cold outside
T rees inside people's houses
M erry Christmas to all of you
A time for joy and celebration
S o merry Christmas everyone!

Tudor Alexandru Timofte (9)
Heene CE (A) Primary School, Worthing

Over The Moon

Excited Lilly building
Ready space pup eating
Amazed Lilly packing
Nervous space pup suiting
Super Lilly suiting too
Everyone is ready
Three, two, one, blast-off!
Scared space pup floating
Suddenly crash
Green alien running
Worried space pup clutching
Boom! They land
Colourful city lighting
Floating cars zooming
Rainbow aliens flying.

Ava B (8)
Ripley Endowed CE Primary School, Ripley

Dwayne

Strong American actor
Bald, brave wrestler
Smart, tall banging
Bald head shining
Enjoy WWE wrestling
All daily training
Dark house knocking
Deep frown watching
Old man scaring
Long legs climbing
Scary freak running.

Albert S (8)
Ripley Endowed CE Primary School, Ripley

School

Happy children playing
White desks sitting
Big board showing
Green reboard looking
Blue chairs sitting
Bronze teacher desk standing
Kind friends playing
Big maths board blue
Silver cloakroom hanging.

Freya Slater (7)
Ripley Endowed CE Primary School, Ripley

Barb The Brave

Speedy boots zooming
Burning eyes blinking
Petite ears listening
Loud voice thundering
Flexible legs turning
Strong arms waving
Shiny sword cutting
Tight belt stretching
Afro hair tangling.

Lewis W (8)
Ripley Endowed CE Primary School, Ripley

Mischievous Fox

Deafening howl screaming
Amber eyes bleeding
Sharp whiskers tickling
Sharp claws scratching
Fluffy fur brushing
Happy tail wagging
Tiny paws scratching.

Olivia P (8)
Ripley Endowed CE Primary School, Ripley

Going To The Park

I like going to the park
To hear laughter filled with fun on slides

I like going to the park
To taste yummy, creamy and mouthwatering ice cream on a hot sunny day

I like going to the park
To touch the sand with my bare hands and make a sandcastle with the soft and velvety sand in the sand pit

I like going to the park
To smell the aroma of the people doing the barbecue

I like going to the park
To look at the sight of the sun setting in burnt orange shades in the sky.

Mariyam Syeda
Smallwood Primary School, Tooting

My Pets

I have a little dog called Daisy
I can see her beautiful brown eyes
I can hear her loud growling
I can smell her smelly breath
I can touch her soft fur
I can taste the cold water that she drinks

I have two cats called Frankie and Paddy
I can see that they like playing with me
I can hear Frankie snoring when he sleeps on my bed
I can smell the disgusting cat treats that Paddy loves
I can touch their fluffy tails
I can taste nothing!

I have three guinea pigs called Tilly, Poppy and Sally
I can hear their little squeaks when they are hungry
I can taste the delicious lettuce they eat
I can smell the fresh vegetables they eat
I can see their tiny bodies squeezing through their little tunnels
I can touch their soft bellies when they sit on me

I love my pets!

Annabelle How (8)
Smallwood Primary School, Tooting

Going To The Beach

Going to the beach
I can see hungry and noisy seagulls gliding above my head
I can see a calm and crystal clear sky like a blue blanket

Going to the beach
I can hear the melody of a delicious ice cream truck
I can hear the roaring and crashing waves breaking on the shore

Going to the beach
I can smell the fragrance of delicious freshly baked chocolate cookies
I can smell the earthy and sometimes funky smell of seaweed

Going to the beach
I can touch the icy cold and wide sea
I can touch soft, silky sand and build sandcastles to play with

Going to the beach
I can taste and sip my delicious, cold and refreshing juice to hydrate my body
I can taste sweet, crispy and yummy waffles to eat as my treat.

Sheema Syeda
Smallwood Primary School, Tooting

Museum To Go!

I can see
I can see
I can see ancient and extinct dinosaur fossils

I can smell
I can smell
I can smell mouthwatering and tummy-grumbling food from the café

I can touch
I can touch
I can touch and feel the historic recreated animal sculpture

I can hear
I can hear
I can hear the sounds of the gigantic roaring animals and the squeaking of tiny creatures

I can taste
I can taste
I can taste the delicious and yummy food that I packed along with me.

Arshiya Syeda
Smallwood Primary School, Tooting

The Dragon Of Fire

I can see a very long dragon
I can see its elongated tail
I can see the dragon breathing out fire

I can hear the dragon roaring
I can hear burning wood
I can hear people screaming

I can feel the dragon breathing on me
I can feel my finger burning
I can feel my clothes on fire

I can smell lots of smoke
I can smell burning wood
I can smell trees on fire

I can taste burning sand flying into my mouth
I can taste smoke
I can taste bits of wood in my mouth.

Ariz Vahora (7)
Smallwood Primary School, Tooting

Cleo

I can see Cleo's small, white belly
I can see her cute nose
I can feel her furry back
I can hear her soft purr
I can hear her tongue cleaning her soft paw
I can smell her in the litter tray from a
mile away
I can feel her soft back
I can almost taste her sweet fur.

Khalid Peart (8)
Smallwood Primary School, Tooting

Spencer The Springer Spaniel

I can see his ears flopping as he runs around
I can hear him rustling in the bushes, hunting for squirrels to chase
I can smell his wet fur from swimming in the rivers
I can taste a juicy sausage as he sniffs around
I can feel his fluffy fur as he lies down.

Oliver Cumming (7)
Smallwood Primary School, Tooting

Chestnut Tree

Tree, tree, my chestnut tree
Trees are short
Trees are tall
Trees are fat
Trees are thin

Under the tree
Finding shade and solace
Under the chestnut tree
Keep calm and enjoy the tranquillity it brings.

Janine Takawira (7)
Smallwood Primary School, Tooting

Christmas Time

I can see the lights on the tree that glow
I can touch fluffy flat snow
I can taste the delicious incredible turkey
I can hear the Christmas songs
I can smell the Brussels sprouts that pong.

Harlow Rodney (8)
Smallwood Primary School, Tooting

Jurassic Coast Fossils

When I go fossil hunting
I can see huge glistening ammonites
I can hear colossal splashing waves
I can smell the dusty rocks
I can taste salty seagrass
I can feel the bumpy ridges of the cliff.

Benedict Lort-Phillips (7)
Smallwood Primary School, Tooting

Halloween

I can taste the delicious pumpkin pie
I can hear the ghosts chattering
I can smell the yummy chocolate
I can see the funny outfits
I can feel the haunted air swooshing around me.

Oliver Gulliford (7)
Smallwood Primary School, Tooting

My Ferocious Cat

I can see a fierce-looking face
I can taste her anger and hate
I can hear her mouth bursting open wide
I can smell her fishy smelly breath
I can feel her pointy teeth and sharp claws.

Sam Marsh (7)
Smallwood Primary School, Tooting

At The Sea

I can taste sweet creamy ice cream
I can smell stinky salty seaweed
I can touch scratchy wet sand
I can see the wavy bubbly sea
I can hear splashing and chatting.

Esme Lewis-Crosby
Smallwood Primary School, Tooting

A Walk In The Park

I can see the trees above.
I can hear the birds chirp.
I can feel the cool grass.
I can smell food from a picnic.
I can taste the picnic food.

Chloe Callaby (7)
Smallwood Primary School, Tooting

Autumn

I can feel the cold breeze
I can hear conkers falling from the tree
I can smell autumn
I can taste hot tomato soup
I can see people wrapped up warmly.

Dylan Ingram-Richardson (7)
Smallwood Primary School, Tooting

My Fan

I can see buttons from one to three
I can smell the fresh air in my face
I can feel the wires of the fan
I can hear the wind blowing.

Iraj Nasir (7)
Smallwood Primary School, Tooting

A Day In The Park

I can see lots of kids in the park
I can hear screaming
I can feel the wet grass
I can taste some food
I can smell some pizza.

Aman Malik (7)
Smallwood Primary School, Tooting

The Angry Cat

I can smell the furious cat
I feel the angry cat
I hear very angry sounds
I taste a feeling
I can touch the smooth angry cat skin.

Kamran Qadeer (7)
Smallwood Primary School, Tooting

My Senses

I can see a book
I can feel the table
I can touch a curve
I can taste seaweed
I can smell the garbage bag.

Kristian Mitrev (7)
Smallwood Primary School, Tooting

A Wondrous Place In The Heart Of The Sea

If you were a bird soaring in the vast sky
What would you see with your wise eyes?
Wild palm trees in the sand
their leaves holding one another's hands
A lonely island standing as still as a statue
Bird poo representing his tattoos
Rough coral talking to the fish
One of the pieces of coral spoke to an eel
with an electric hiss
Fresh air blowing through your feathers
At this point, there are no worries, never.

Kamva Sowati (9)
St Mary's CE (VA) Primary School, Portbury

The Eagle's Adventure!

If you were a bird soaring in the vast sky
What would you see with your wise eye?
Buildings as tall as skyscrapers shining in
the sun
Deserts as hot as flames that cook you like
a bun
Trees as green as grass swaying in
the breeze
Oceans as blue as whales with no sign of
any trees
A silent dark night where your mum says
goodnight.

Josh Jenkins (9)
St Mary's CE (VA) Primary School, Portbury

The Hooting Owl

If you were a bird soaring in the vast sky
What would you see with your wise eyes?
The calming sky as calming as swaying trees
The freezing air is as freezing as snow
The bright moon is as bright as the sun
The rough branches as rough as a log
The fresh grass is like a fresh salad.

Rebecca Poole (8)
St Mary's CE (VA) Primary School, Portbury

Pog The Dog

I have a dog
He is called Pog.
When we planted a tree
He barked at it with glee.
I love the tree
And he loves me.
We sing
And sometimes use a ring.
We planted the tree in Portbury.
One day we lost Pog
In the fog.
Pog found the tree
And he found me.

Seb Johnson (7)
St Mary's CE (VA) Primary School, Portbury

Island Of Fun

If you were a bird soaring in the vast sky
What would you see with your wise eyes?
Have you heard of the Island of Fun
Where there's a house made of candy
Mountains that scrape the sky
Plus you have little mountains if you start small
You'll always see a rainbow.

Jacob Baylis (7)
St Mary's CE (VA) Primary School, Portbury

Beach Poem

I see the deep blue sea as blue as the sky
A bright sun as yellow as a sunflower
I see bright green grass
I see grey singing slides
I see the sand that is gold
I see a boat sailing toward me
I see an ice cream truck heading towards me
I see the light blue sea.

Shana Bateman (7)
St Mary's CE (VA) Primary School, Portbury

Space Is Out Of This World

Space has stars and twinkles
The stars are bright at night
I love space because it is wonderful
In space, there are lots of colours
The colours in space are beautiful and incredible
Space is out of this world
Can you see the colours in space?
The sky is pretty.

Imogen Speed (5)
St Mary's CE (VA) Primary School, Portbury

The Mermaids

In the deep sea, the mermaids live
They live in a water cave
They will not go on land
They have a pet called Snowflake
Snowflake is a cat
They also have a pet axolotl
They like to swim in the sea
Fish jump in and out
They like to jump too and they twirl.

Eva Ahern (6)
St Mary's CE (VA) Primary School, Portbury

Soaring Through The Sky!

If you were a bird soaring in the vast sky
What would you see with your wise eyes?
Fluffy clouds are as white as the moon
Icy mountains are as soft as sugar powder
Calm mountain goats bleating as quietly as a mouse
The fresh air is as fresh as the river.

Sebastian Purcell (8)
St Mary's CE (VA) Primary School, Portbury

Rooby

Rooby likes to dance and sing
Rooby is playful
She will always help
Rooby is cute and fun
Rooby is stripy and fluffy
She likes to play with her friends
Her friends are Esme and Devon
They play together at break
They play with a ball.

Esme Smith (6)
St Mary's CE (VA) Primary School, Portbury

Superhero Girl

Don't mess with Supergirl
Supergirl is powerful
She is pretty
She is good at fighting
She is stronger than you
She is good at stopping a train
She is the best superhero in the whole entire world
She is great like Miss Cree.

Charlie Ferguson (6)
St Mary's CE (VA) Primary School, Portbury

Beach Summer Day

If you were a bird soaring in the vast sky
What would you see with your wise eyes?
The beach is as warm as an ocean
The rocks are as icy as the North Pole
The sand is as scorching as the sun
The enormous dazzling air with fluffy clouds.

Marika Korbien (8)
St Mary's CE (VA) Primary School, Portbury

What Can You See?

If you were a bird soaring in the vast sky
What would you see with your wise eyes?
Brown water rushing as fast as a car
Traffic beeping as loud as a lion
Purple hot air balloons rising like the sun
Chains clanking like a crane.

Jacob Thomson (8)
St Mary's CE (VA) Primary School, Portbury

Forbidden Falls

If you were a bird soaring in the vast sky
What would you see with your wise eyes?
The lush breeze on your wings
The rushing waterfall, Forbidden Falls
A lush place to be
A nice breeze carrying you away from the lush place.

Charlotte Corr (9)
St Mary's CE (VA) Primary School, Portbury

The Bird

If you were a bird soaring in the vast sky
What would you see with your wise eyes?
Acorns are as brown as a tree
The moon is as dark as an elephant
The grass is as fresh as a new tree
The sky is as freezing as an ice cube.

Emilia Bundy (7)
St Mary's CE (VA) Primary School, Portbury

The Ezra Poem

If you were a bird soaring in the vast sky
What would you see with your wise eyes?
Spikey, narrow, sharp acorns
Narrow cliffs like a leather box
Amazing long spikes as sharp as a knife
Small spikes like a lion's teeth.

Ezra Jones (7)
St Mary's CE (VA) Primary School, Portbury

Miss Cree

Miss Cree is very nice
Because she helps Windmill Class
She helps people when they are stuck
She sometimes plays in PE
She does a cheesy smile
Sometimes she tells some jokes
And Windmill Class laugh a big loud laugh.

Freya Larder (6)
St Mary's CE (VA) Primary School, Portbury

The Wonderful Star

The star is twinkly
The star is small
The star is yellow
The star only comes out at night
The star is wonderful
The star is beautiful
The star is very high
The star is happy
The star is shiny.

Lochy Batt (5)
St Mary's CE (VA) Primary School, Portbury

The Beautiful Beach Of Flamingos

If you were a bird soaring in the vast sky
What would you see with your wise eyes?
A wavy blue sea waving in the wind
A yellow sandy beach as sandy as a pot
I love the beach so much
It is so much fun.

Amelia Burke (7)
St Mary's CE (VA) Primary School, Portbury

Lilly's Diary

Lilly the unicorn had a diary
Lilly took the diary everywhere
She loved her diary
She loved it so much
She took it to the farm
Where it was muddy and sludgy
She loved her diary a lot.

Bella Poole (6)
St Mary's CE (VA) Primary School, Portbury

Tom The Superhero

Tom is cuddly
Tom is powerful
Tom is good
Tom is nice and he never gives up
He is fearful and listens very well
He is a superhero
He saves the day
He is strong and helpful.

Devon Dempsey (6)
St Mary's CE (VA) Primary School, Portbury

Spices The Great Dragon

This is Spices the dragon
He is fast
He likes lamb
Don't mess with Spices
He likes a fight
For he lives in a cave
You may think he is dead
But he is okay.

Arran Batt (6)
St Mary's CE (VA) Primary School, Portbury

If You Were A Bird...

If you were a bird soaring in the vast sky
What would you see with your wise eyes?
I would see a high hill
And some cars
A gargantuan building
And a bright green tree.

Max Hill (8)
St Mary's CE (VA) Primary School, Portbury

What Can You See?

A wavy ocean as blue as the sky on a sunny day
The yellow sun as bright as a bright light
A white cloud as white as a swan
A black penguin as black as coal.

Edith Dean (7)
St Mary's CE (VA) Primary School, Portbury

The Police Chase

Fast police car is trying to get the robber
The sirens light up to make the car faster
And they catch the car
They put the robber in jail.

Saul Chalkley (6)
St Mary's CE (VA) Primary School, Portbury

Paradise

If you were a bird soaring in the vast sky
What would you see with your wise eyes?
A plain paradise
With lots of sand and water.

Lamar Ali (9)
St Mary's CE (VA) Primary School, Portbury

Snowy Mountains

The mountains were as snowy as a snowstorm
The clouds were white as shiny silk paper
The mountains were as cold as a freezer.

Max Joyner (7)
St Mary's CE (VA) Primary School, Portbury

Bil

Bil has a tail
Bil has big legs
Bil has big spikes
Bil has a big head
Bil has big eyes
Bil has a big tummy.

Aneirin Guttridge (5)
St Mary's CE (VA) Primary School, Portbury

Layla Morgan

L ollies are the best in the world
A lligators are the best in the world because they are sly
Y elling at my brother is what I like to do
L aughing with my friends makes me happy
A pples are delicious, I eat them every day

M arching with my friend is fun
O ctopuses are cool
R ed is the colour of my uniform
G rowling is the best in the world
A nimals are so cute
N urses are caring because they help people get better.

Layla Morgan (7)
St Wilfrid's Catholic Primary School, Ashton In Makerfield

My Name

M y mum is 27
I n winter, it's my birthday
A lligators are cool

P eople that are kind get toys
A kid is fun, like me
S top littering
Q uirky people are interesting
U neven paths are hard to walk on
I n my room, there is a big spider
L aughing is happiness
L ast week, I was not allowed my iPad.

Mia Pasquill (6)
St Wilfrid's Catholic Primary School, Ashton In Makerfield

Nice Lucy

L ook at this, it's my favourite food ever
U nder the stairs is where I put my shoes
C an you see my best talent?
Y ou are my best friend

J oshua is my brother and he is the best
A n ice cream is nice and I love it
N ana is the best and I love her
E very day I go to school to see my friends.

Lucy Carson (6)
St Wilfrid's Catholic Primary School, Ashton In Makerfield

Ben The Best

B ooks are the best to read
E aster is the best time of the year
N uts are the worst
J am is the best on toast and croissants
A ll my family are the best
M y mum is the best for snuggling
I n my house is my dog that I love
N o one is better than my family.

Benjamin Pennington (6)
St Wilfrid's Catholic Primary School, Ashton In Makerfield

Kangaroo In A Race

K angaroos are my favourite animal
S nakes are very long and slimy
A t my football club, we always win
W ebs are a spider's home
I t is cool when my grandma comes
E lephants are the heaviest animal on land
R acing is the best for me because I'm really fast.

Ksawier Pitucha (7)
St Wilfrid's Catholic Primary School, Ashton In Makerfield

Cool Kasper

K angaroos are medium-sized
A pples are good to eat
S nakes can be longer than a skipping rope
P alm oil is not good for the environment
E lephants are bigger than a house
R abbits have big ears that flap when they jump.

Kasper Ballard (6)
St Wilfrid's Catholic Primary School, Ashton In Makerfield

Fire Freddie

F riends are the best
R oko is gone and I love him
E very day I have fun at school
D ays at school are fun
D ays are the best days ever
I like to go to the beach
E very day I like to go to gymnastics.

Freddie Ballard (6)
St Wilfrid's Catholic Primary School, Ashton In Makerfield

Olivia's Life

O rangutans are the best animals
L ove is the best thing you can have
I ndulgent cakes are tasty to eat
V ans are great for a ride in
I nteresting days are spent on the farm
A nimals are the cutest in the world.

Olivia Smith (6)
St Wilfrid's Catholic Primary School, Ashton In Makerfield

A Little Bit About Me

M y favourite colour is red
A friend is important to have
S ome of my favourite sports are football and rugby
O n Friday, I have McDonald's and I love it
N o one is as great as a teacher as Jesus.

Mason Olori (6)
St Wilfrid's Catholic Primary School, Ashton In Makerfield

Fire Strike

L ook at all the sunflowers in the field
O n Sunday, I play rugby with my friends
G old is my favourite colour
A pples are my favourite fruit
N ew puppies are cute, I really want one for my birthday.

Logan Sheridan (6)
St Wilfrid's Catholic Primary School, Ashton In Makerfield

Ella's Special Things

E lephants are the animals that I like best
L ove making crafts for my family and friends
L ovely days out are good, especially with my mummy and me
A lways showing care and love to my family.

Ella Easton (6)
St Wilfrid's Catholic Primary School, Ashton In Makerfield

My Life

S un is always bright
Y oyos are my favourite
L orries are big and like a truck
V iolet is my favourite colour
I love chocolate
E lsie is my cousin.

Sylvie Smith (6)
St Wilfrid's Catholic Primary School, Ashton In Makerfield

Out Of Space

B ecause I was bored with a toy, I put it in the bin
L ick an ice cream
A BC is the best song
K ick a ball in football
E ek at vampires because they are creepy!

Blake Thorpe (6)
St Wilfrid's Catholic Primary School, Ashton In Makerfield

Molly

M y favourite animal is a turtle
O rangutans are so cute
L aughing is so much fun
L oving marshmallows is what I do
Y ellow jelly is the best thing ever!

Molly Armstrong-Storey (6)
St Wilfrid's Catholic Primary School, Ashton In Makerfield

Waffles

L oving and caring is how people describe me
E ntertaining times are with my brother, Isaac
O ften I play on games, my favourite one is Slime Rancher!

Leo Stott (6)
St Wilfrid's Catholic Primary School, Ashton In Makerfield

YOUNG WRITERS INFORMATION

We hope you have enjoyed reading this book – and that you will continue to in the coming years.

If you're the parent or family member of an enthusiastic poet or story writer, do visit our website **www.youngwriters.co.uk/subscribe** and sign up to receive news, competitions, writing challenges and tips, activities and much, much more! There's lots to keep budding writers motivated!

If you would like to order further copies of this book, or any of our other titles, then please give us a call or order via your online account.

Young Writers
Remus House
Coltsfoot Drive
Peterborough
PE2 9BF
(01733) 890066
info@youngwriters.co.uk

Join in the conversation!
Tips, news, giveaways and much more!

YoungWritersUK   YoungWritersCW   youngwriterscw